Observe the wonders as they occur around us.   –Rumi

The Poetry of Rumi

An Illustrated Journal

You are a song, a wished-for song. Move to the center, towards the sky and wind, towards silent knowing.

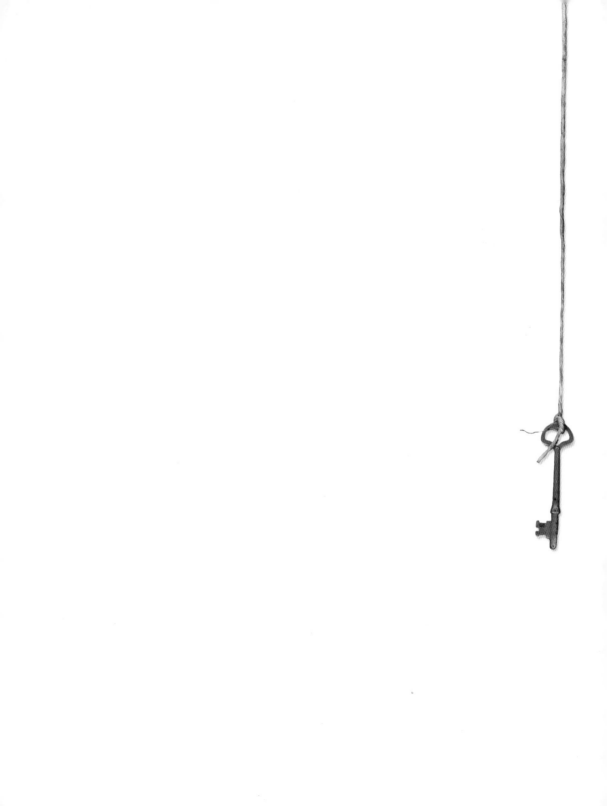

This is the purpose of emotion, to let a streaming beauty flow through you.

The most lasting moment comes when those who love each other meet each other's eyes and in what flows between them.

There is one who can help, who turns the wheel from non-existence to a sweet breathing emptiness.

Everything you want and need is inside you.

Make me sweet again, fragrant and fresh and wild, and thankful for any small event.

When you do things from your soul, you feel a river moving in you, a joy.

The way

the night

knows

itself

with

the moon,

be that

with me.

When wisdom transforms the senses,   you will s and feel whose words fall away and whose remain inside you to guide.

Don't grieve. Anything you lose comes around in another form.

Love so vast,

love the sky

cannot contain!

How does

all this

fit within

my heart?

The light changes. I need more grace than I thought.

Your graceful manner gives color and fragrance.

This moment is all there is.

The breeze at dawn has secrets to tell you. You must ask for what you really want.

See beyond phenomena and these difficult questions

will dissolve into love within love.

The heart is the wheat grain.   *We are the mill.*

The

rose's

rarest

essence

lives

in the

thorn.

You have

a source

inside you,

a cool spring.

Something opens our wings. Something makes boredom and hurt disappear

Someone fills the cup in front of us. We taste only sacredness.

Be ground. Be crumbled so wild flowers will come up where you are.

There

is a

path

from

me to you

that

I am

constantly

looking

for.

Keep
knocking
and the
joy
inside
will
eventually
open
a window
and
look
out
to see
who's
there.

Whenever some kindness comes to you, turn that way, toward the source of kindness.

All religions, all this singing, is one song. The differences are just illusion and vanity.

A candle

is made

to become

entirely

flame,

a tongue

of light

describing

a refuge.

The inner secret, that which was never born, you are that freshness, and I am with you now.

No matter

we're

in a

prison of

forgetting

or enjoying

the banquet

of wisdom.

We are

always

inside

presence.

You

are a

song,

a wished-

for

song.

Move

to the

center,

towards

the sky

and wind,

towards

silent

knowing.

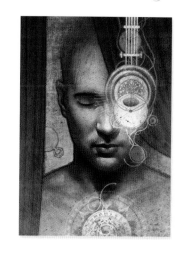

The breeze at dawn has secrets to tell you. You must ask for what you really want.

Tend to your vital heart, and all your worry will be dissolved.

We are the night ocean filled with glints of light.

We listen to words so we can silently reach into the other.

Look for the answer inside your question.

Be

courageous

and

discipline

yourself.

Work.

Keep

digging

your

well.

Water

is

there

somewhere.

The only lasting beauty is the beauty of the heart.

As
essence
turns
to ocean
the
particles
glisten.
Watch
how
in this
candle
flame
instant.
Blaze
all
the
moments
you
have
lived.

The inner secret, that which was never born, you are that freshness, and I am with you now.

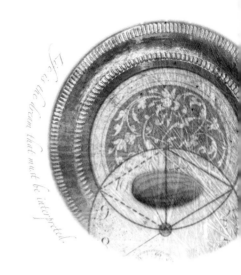

Life is like a dream that must be interpreted.

The poetry of Rumi, written nearly 800 years ago, opens the mystery of the world, the mystery and sacredness of our lives.

Jelaluddin Rumi was born in Balkh, Afghanistan, then part of the Persian Empire, in 1207. Fleeing the threat of invading Mongol armies, his family emigrated to Konya, Turkey, a city where Muslim, Christian, Hindu and Buddhist travelers mingled. There, Rumi met a wandering dervish named Shams of Tabriz, who became his teacher and spiritual companion. Their meeting altered the course of Rumi's life, and thus our lives today. Rumi's passionate, playful poems celebrate the sacredness of everyday life and illuminate its deepest mysteries.

Coleman Barks is regarded as the world's premier translator of Rumi's writing. His translations of Rumi have now sold a half a million copies. The father of two grown children and grandfather of four, he has retired from university teaching.

Matt Manley is a painter and digital artist. His work brings together painting, found objects, textures and photographs that form a beautiful and mystical union with the words of Rumi.

All artwork by Matt Manley
All translations by Coleman Barks
Book design by Liz Kalloch